EMRE AROLAT SCENT OF THE TRACE

Introduction by Aaron Betsky

Scent of the Trace

4	Order, Barely: The Architecture of Emre Arolat Aaron Betsky
10	Scent of the Trace Emre Arolat
34	Bergama Cultural Center
62	Sancaklar Mosque
90	Yalıkavak Marina
118	Appendix

Order, Barely: The Architecture of Emre Arolat

Aaron Betsky

To arrive at the Sancaklar Mosque in the far suburbs of Istanbul, on a hill scoured by wind overlooking what remains of the rolling pastures now disappearing under gated developments and highways tying together this ever-growing metropolis, is to find a moment of clarity. All you see is a few walls – one vertical, a few horizontal. They are covered in stones set loosely on top of each other, flinty and raw like the place. You might encounter a cow wandering through the space. Next door, another subdivision is under construction. Distracted, you stub your toe on a stone, look down, find another stone lower than that, follow it down, and soon find yourself racing down the hill, past a tumulus of more of those same fragments of the earth, that bulges with the weight of the hill.

You arrive at a clearing sheltered from the winds. Now the walls are concrete, and roofs jut out, indicating respite. You move past the walls, find yourself inside, wash your feet, your hands, and your face, and then proceed into the mosque. As you enter, the space opens up. It is a cave carved into the hill. The floor falls away and you find yourself facing a concrete plane, washed by light from above. A niche indicates the direction to which you should pray. A spill of steps next to that indication of a Mihrab allows the Imam to speak to you. The ceiling above you disappears as layers carved into the soil. That is all. You have found a place for the spirit. It is also a site of otherness and separation, of peace, of focus, and of community.

Few architects combine order and sensuality to greater effect than Emre Arolat does. Working with geometries that distinguish themselves through their simplicity and a palette that rarely consists of more than concrete, wood, glass, and stone, he is able to achieve effects that make full use of the sites his buildings occupy, while respecting the restraints that constrain his ability to be fully expressive.

This is not to say that Arolat and his firm EAA, have not been given opportunities that any other architect would envy. It is also not to say that some of the firm's projects are as glitzy and banal as those of many other corporate firms. Yet, through its position among the most successful firms in a country whose economic growth has been remarkable for the last decade, EAA has received commissions for large commercial projects, luxury housing, and cultural structures in locations and with circumstances that let Arolat use the layers of history of which Anatolia's legacy consists to make a bare and beautiful order. It is exactly the combination of restraint and relish in the possibilities these opportunities have afforded him that makes his architecture so successful.

Arolat works do not necessarily refer to specific local traditions or forms, nor does he try to create the attractors for global capital that could appear anywhere. He instead searches for ways to make buildings that have a particular solidity and clarity that make sense of their position, while operating within the standards and according to the codes that ensure his work is successful, both in a financial sense and in terms of the taste culture within which he operates.

Certainly, Arolat continues the particular traditions of building within Turkey. These include both the attention to proportion and sequence that marked the glory of Ottoman architecture, but have also developed on the fascination with the potential of concrete frames that made Turkey the construction engine of the Middle East and beyond and disciplined the work of Arolat's teachers. Turkey has long adopted and adapted foreign influences, both as imperial overlords assimilating other cultures and as a country looking to western forms and styles. It has only been in the last generation that architects—as well as artists—have tried to figure out what might be particular to their situation within a global economy and culture.

Sancaklar Mosque

The most important aspect of that situation for architects is the boom in construction both in Turkey itself, and in the export of design and building that made Turkey a major provider of such services in the Middle East, parts of the former Soviet Union, and Africa: in 2017, Turkey ranked second in the world for the export of such expertise (behind China) for the tenth year in the row. When Turkish construction companies went to build in other countries, they often brought their architects with them, and a network of connections followed. As a result, Arolat has worked around those areas, and is now expanding into the United States.

Moreover, the boom in economic conditions in general until 2018 led to an explosion of wealth that, in combination with the grandiose ambitions of the Erdogan regime, resulted in the construction of both large private projects—such as the sort of mixed-use apartment building, office tower, and shopping mall structures of which Arolat has designed some of the best—and public projects, ranging from roads and airports to mosques and community centers. Although centered on Istanbul, such construction spread at least through the eastern part of Anatolia and around the major cities. It is difficult to visit Bodrum, a small fishing village a few decades ago that is now a major hub on the international yacht and vacation home circuit (and where Arolat has also built several of his best projects) and not marvel at emergence of Turkey into the realm rich—and wasteful and economically deeply divided—countries.

left Modulations in the façade of St. Regis
below Oval cove in the ceiling of St. Regis hotel room

While the sheer volume of construction has been prodigious, the quality of the architecture has not always kept pace. The design of most of the large—and small—new projects in Turkey in recent years has been no better or worse than the mean in the rest of the world, which is to say exorable. The good pieces of architecture therefore stand out, especially when they make use of the available technologies, which in Turkey means concrete frames. The expression and manipulation of such frames has become the mainstay of Arolat's architecture.

This concentration is not just a reaction to building traditions, however. It is also both an aesthetic choice and a continuation of the work of some of the best and most idiosyncratic designers of the previous generations of Turkish architects, such as Sedad Hakki Eldem and Turgut Cansever, both of whose work Arolat particularly admires and in whose footsteps he seeks to work. The prevalence of three-dimensional grids, the expression of concrete floors, and the sequencing of spaces ordered by such overall framing devices, is central to this tradition. If one stretches even further, one can find the roots of such a focus not only in building traditions, available materials, and the ways in which architects of the post-Ottoman period reacted to them, but also in the architecture produced at height of Ottoman power, and in particular in the rhythms and near perfect proportions evident in the work of Mimar Sinan and other mosque builders of that period.

What Arolat has added to these conditions and traditions is a particular interest in the slipping and sliding of planes, as well as the curving or cutting of spaces, that modulates the orders he establishes as the first facts of his projects. After setting up grids, often with columns or blocks, he then cuts through them, usually not with literal diagonals or curves, but more often through implications and sequence. You move through his projects on a diagonal as you are guided by sequences of walls that shift and fade, guiding, rather than pointing you on your ways. Modulations in the façade, whether through shutters that open and close in many of his housing and hotel projects, or through slight movements of balconies, ledges, or even ceiling details, further open up and agitate the framed blocks. I first became aware of this motif as I lay in bed in my room at the St. Regis Istanbul, staring up at the oval cove, set at a diagonal, in the ceiling. I found out later it indicates the movement Arolat intended between the two flanking streets that meet at a sharp angle at the far end of the building.

One can see all these aspects of Arolat's work on display in the three projects on which this volume focuses. Though all three are among his smaller designs, they are quite different in their function (commercial, religious, and mixed commercial and cultural) and their locations. They also typify the particular situations in which EAA had the opportunity to express the core of their approach.

The Marina at Yalıkavak in Bodrum is both the most extensive and the most compromised of the three. Since its completion in 2014, it has suffered from additions and alternations that have compromised the clarity and purity of Arolat's original intentions. In particular, the horizontality of the project, so essential for it both to act as a mediation between land and water, and to create an order that is meant to contain the many messages that are proper to stores, restaurants, and bars, has to some extent fallen apart through the creation of second floor pavilions, railings, and other vertical extensions.

The beauty of the project is the economy of its means. It consists of an agglomeration of planes, columns, and intersections, some of which enclose stores or restaurants, others of which mark corners or turning points, and yet others of which extend to enclose or screen off larger structures, such as the marina service area and a small hotel. Clad in a local stone, these structuring elements are smooth and abstract, standing between the vertical lines of the jagged mountains and hills behind and beyond them and the surface of the sea to which they answer.

The main function of the walls is to screen and de-limit: they are the boundaries of the project towards its rear, and provide the dividing point between service and public, while also acting as a backdrop to the activities that take place within them. Yet they are also more than that. They guide you along your way, extending out to make paths and pointing towards the next cluster of activity.

At times, the walls do come together to create a larger grouping of structures, especially on the artificial island that is the project's most isolated and three-dimensional complex area. There, the volumes containing the functions make themselves known, giving a solidity to the continual extension of the rest of the project. At other times, the walls disappear behind such screening devices as the tree branches Arolat uses to give both privacy and a dappled light to the hotel rooms. What makes the project work successfully is the rhythm of open and closed, continuation and solidification, order and fluidity, that dissolves what would otherwise be a rather large development.

The detailing Arolat uses here as elsewhere serves that purpose. In some parts of the projects, that choice of the meeting place of materials emphasizes the continuation of planes: glass walls disappear into soffits, while the planes of the floor continue to, and then slightly over the edges of pools. At other places, it is the mass that predominates, with the stone cladding wrapping around columns and corners to give you a sense that this an object, but an abstract one; it is a statement of intent rather than just the result of the building process.

The result is a response to the landscape of rough, dry hills and choppy, wind-swept water. The marina buildings catch that context, not only in reflections, but also in the ways in which the project mirrors and twists those forms to find the planes and masses within them. It is not only a response to nature, however. It is also a modern version of a Kasbah, or of the small fishing villages clustering along the bays and inlet of the area. Neither contextual nor vernacular, the Yalıkavak Marina is modern Turkey on the water, at play and yet fully aware of its place and culture.

The site Arolat faced in Bergama, on the other hand, was considerably more laden—at least in terms of human presence—than that in Bodrum. The city was once called Pergamum and was one of the largest and most important sites of the Hellenistic era. On the hill overlooking what is now a small agricultural trading town you can still find the ruins of the acropolis, even if the Zeus Temple—its crowning glory—is now languishing in Berlin. The temples lining up along both solar and local landscape axes, the theater plunging down the slope, and the arrangement of stoas and walkways that connected these cultural and religious structures are still visible, if only in traces, both there and nearer to the project's site in the ruins of the Asklepion, or former hospital.

The Cultural Center is a homage and a rethinking of that acropolis. Instead of just connecting or lining the central buildings, however, the arcades here ring them completely. They form a buffer to the confusion of the town all around it, ordering its rhythms into even bays set back far enough from the main street leading towards the old town to allow for a pedestrian presence around the development. They also contain the commercial activities of the small stores and restaurants, becoming a place of connection, shade, and just hanging out, whether to drink a cup of coffee or to check your cellphone. Deep and strong, the arcades assert themselves as the major presence and identity of the Cultural Center, leaping over the street in a bridge that connects the neighborhood to the west that sits on a slight rise above the rest of the town.

Once you pass through the arcades, you find yourself in a world of alternating sun and shade, open and closed rooms, and commercial and cultural functions, all organized around small courtyards that are large enough to invite human activity, but not so extensive as to become fully formed spaces in themselves. Arolat has not only subverted the project's commercial components, but has done the same with the theaters, library, and small exhibition space that make up the Cultural Center's core. You can never get far enough away from any of them to see them to their fullest extent, let alone to be as impressed by them as a such monument usually asks you to be. At most, you sense the barren, unadorned concrete masses peaking up above the layers of arcades and bridges, or you can look down at them huddled inside those layers from the western hill. Even then, the largest of all them turns into a screen for outdoor movie showings, while the seating takes over the roof of the library.

Arolat has also worked hard to prevent the emergence of any central axis or clear geometry. This is a theme in his work that he here uses with much success in his larger projects, where the continual weaving and twisting of directions breaks down their often immense scale, so that you continually slide by the large masses, circulating away and along them, without approaching what should be the development's core elements head-on. The downside of this approach is a certain amount of confusion, but that lack of clarity also serves to confront and weave together the sacred and the profane, the commercial movie theaters and the home for the local theater company, the coffee shop and the heavily used library.

It is, in fact, a tribute to the success of Arolat's approach that the Cultural Center is crawling with people, even during the day, when the largest masses, those of the performance and cinema halls, are empty of activity. People use the space, above all else, the way they do the small streets and squares, none of them straight or orthogonal, that make up the nearby old city: to be together. If the acropolis once served to stand above and provide order to Pergamum, the Bergama Cultural Center now serves to integrate and provide and anchor to the much more modest urban area. It is, like most of Arolat's work, a collection of ruins of monuments, ordered versions of the surroundings, simple backdrops to human activities, and walls and walkways that guide you along through these building blocks of a contemporary collective.

The exception to such strategies or urban mixing and framing is the Sancaklar Mosque. It is completely removed from the neighborhoods around it, and its central space is remarkable in the grandeur that it achieves for a prayer hall that seats no more than a few hundred congregants. This is, of course, because this is a religious structure, and one in a context that provides few of the clues or relations that the settings of the other projects afford. What Arolat does instead is to establish the project's own place. What is the same here as it is in the architecture of many of the other of EAA's portfolio is that Arolat dissolves the whole structure into a series of walkways, walls, and the experiences that they create.

In this case, those building blocks are not the smooth and finished forms you see in many of his other projects, but structures clad in stone that is loosely stacked with no mortar. This gives these walls a more primitive character, bringing to mind both ancient farm buildings, huts, and field walls, and the menhirs and markers that once designated places of significance. Arolat uses similar materials on the sides of some of his residential structures, where they serve to blend these new buildings into the surrounding landscape, but here the dividers stand all by themselves, making an implied and open space.

The place they shape is available for outdoor worship, but also for livestock to graze or for anybody to rest and survey the landscape in the shelter from the wind the structures provide. At the lower level, the walls line up both to enclose the library and office space that faces the worship room across a small plaza, and to screen off the ablution area. It is only when you move into the porch and then into the prayer hall that the piles of stone disappear completely, giving way to the carpet and smooth walls that create the womb of community. Even here, though, some of the hill, the earth, and the tomb are present in the jagged ridges Arolat cut into the ceiling to denote the central space and provide lighting. The Sancaklar Mosque moves beyond the present day, but also beyond order and day-to-day functions. It retreats back into the earth in a way the more mundane projects in Bodrum and Bergama, let alone the large shopping centers and housing projects his office has produced, never could.

Though it would be easy to assume, therefore, that the mosque, and subsequent religious projects that have followed its popular and critical success, is at the core of Arolat's architecture. I would not be so sure. He is not a religious man and, what is even more important, his projects seem to do best when they hover at the edge of meaning and mass, monumentality and abstract order, and the confusion and mix of everyday life. In this best work, you often find that whenever he states an order, he breaks it. He cannot even repeat himself in modules, as his office has found out when they ask him to standardize layouts for multi-unit housing projects and he instead reinvents the form of every single one of the living areas. When he makes tall towers, he dissolves them into the horizontal striations of Zorlu project or breaks them apart into the off-kilter blocks of the Heyat Park Mixed Use Complex. When he does make a single block, as in the St. Regis Hotel, he hides it behind shutters whose configuration changes continually. He tries to fit into the hillsides where he builds luxury houses in Bodrum, saving every tree he can and nestling the structures next to and top of each other, rather than in straight lines. Even when he designs a large space of cultural importance, such as the performance hall at Zorlu, he makes it almost invisible from the outside and makes its foyer into an outdoor space where you can watch soccer matches as well as wait for the show to start.

Perhaps the archetypal Arolat project will be the just-opened hotel in Antakya (the ancient Antioch). Hovering over archeological ruins through which its structure weaves, it extends into courtyards and walkways connecting the various rooms and service functions. It provides a sense of place and builds itself up out of both the necessary structure and the ancient foundation, and then never coheres, but only extends into something new, something sheltered, something that barely states itself. One can find something similar in the scheme for the Museum of Painting and Sculpture in Istanbul, a reworking and opening up of an old warehouse. This is where Arolat's architecture is located: suspended between so many things that make up what Turkey and he have become and where they are going.

This is also exactly what makes Arolat and his team so good. They are able to find just enough of a sense of coherence and fit just enough into tradition, commercial norms, and building norms, to be able to eke out something that keeps going, slides away, slips into a small place of gathering, layers itself into either the urban or the natural landscape, and makes a place where you want to sit to watch the view, other people, or the presence of divinity.

top Antakya Museum Hotel interior shot showing the ruins and the restaurant
above Antakya Museum Hotel exterior shot showing the modular rooms

Scent of the Trace

Emre Arolat

Well Now, Just the Sort of Project You Wanted!

It's been more than eight years... We were still in the Etiler office.[1] Finally winter's last freeze. Bright sun licks the chalk-white roofs in spite of the storm outside. Istanbul is even more beautiful after a snowfall...

I think to myself how young he is to be a mayor. A smiling, sparkling clean-cut young man. He chooses his words carefully. Very polite. After a brief preamble, he gets straight to the point.

"I read your recent interview in the Art and Culture section of Radikal newspaper.[2] First of all, I would like to congratulate you on winning the Aga Khan Award for Architecture.[3] You have made us all proud. Yet that is not the real reason I called you and came to your office. As I said on the phone, I have been serving as Mayor of Bergama Municipality[4] for almost nine months. We have initiated important projects in this period. And, the people of Bergama have given us their enthusiastic support."

"We have a prime piece of land at the city center. A site of some 7,500 square meters. Today it is in a terrible state, occupied by makeshift shops. We want to create there the sort of center the city has long felt to be lacking, a public space devoted mainly to culture and the arts. We are thinking that a certain amount of commercial space may be added to the project as well. Our intention is not to completely displace the shopkeepers but rather provide them with higher quality spaces."

"By now you must have understood why I am here. I want very much to design this project with an architect such as yourself. In your newspaper interview, you said that the public sector avoids employing quality architect services, and generally runs such projects through old boy networks. From what I read I even concluded that you were a bit annoyed at not being able to participate in such public projects. But here you have before you the opportunity to do public design in precisely the sense you meant. I must add right away that we do not have a large budget to devote to our project services. Still, if you will help us out in this regard, we would like to have you as our guest in Bergama. See the site. Let us really show you our city."

As I exit the airport terminal a few weeks later I am met by the sweet scent of the Aegean. A black vehicle with government plates is waiting for me across from the exit. A driver wearing a suit emerges from the car and says, *"My Mayor regrets he was not able to come to meet you personally."* I certainly did not expect such a thing. The drive from Izmir to Bergama is an hour and a half. The weather is delicious. Once we have escaped the city traffic the landscape changes completely. We seem to flow through a great banquet of vegetation all along the road north.

I visited Bergama and its Acropolis as a child. The truth is my path had not led me there again. What stayed in my mind was a huge hill topped by the ruins of the ancient city. I remember being impressed most of all by the amphitheater on the slope. I absolutely must go there again. As for the new city, I have almost no memory of it.

The Atatürk Boulevard originating in the southwest stretches toward the city center and runs without a break all along the town. It narrows toward the north where the surrounding settlement is more built up. It starts as the Boulevard of the Republic and becomes Banks Boulevard. Almost all the important structures of the city are on this road.

As soon as we pass the stadium we pull over alongside makeshift structures lining the road. Most are one-story high. Dust everywhere. The Mayor comes toward me accompanied by the few people with him. He has that same sparkling smile on his face. One by one he introduces the technicians who will work on this municipal project, giving their names and positions.

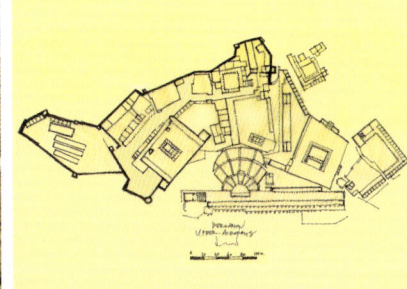

above The mayor and the bazaar of Bergama
left The acropolis, Pergamon the old amphitheater, Emre Arolat's simplified plan of upper acropolis of Pergamon
below The acropolis from the new city

above and right The new city from the acropolis
left Pergamon the old city

I suppose "place" and "context" in the broadest sense are the most important issues in my adventure in architecture. *"Like we do, you favor an interpretivist approach,"* Murat Güvenç said once during one of our long, enjoyable conversations years ago.[5] For a time at METU,[6] they used to call a group of academics of which he was a part "interpretivists." He talked about these things in an ironic way. It's strange, I never forgot it and have thought of myself like that ever since.

Interpretivist... to understand. To try to understand. To try every possible way of doing that. To make a curve when necessary, to look at a place from above, or along the surface, or from below. Or to consider a context, a situation, from every angle. To go all the way to the bottom, even inside, or if necessary stand all the way back to see how it looks from there. To listen. To listen intently to every whisper. To breathe in deeply the scents that traces give off. It is actually a kind of process of intellectual discovery. A path not content with the merely physical, with appearances and what can easily be pointed out. To search mercilessly, unable to stop until the thing has been worked out. For me, design has always and in every circumstance corresponded to "that specific condition" I struggle to understand, comprehend, and as much as possible internalize.

We wander all over the city, exploring nooks and crannies. The central market is full of life. Weaving and kilim arts are practiced widely here. Colorfully patterned textiles are carefully arranged in shop windows. Shopkeepers make the best possible use of external space. And the climate is favorable, of course. Whatever else, this is an Aegean settlement. It is clear that the people here have enjoyed spending time out of doors since the days of ancient Pergamon. Some things never change. Whether it is a great city with magnificent monuments, even the splendid seat of a kingdom, or as it is today a much more humble county, the same wind blows here. Whether the inhabitants are Ionian or Roman, the sun warms it now just as it did in the seventh-century B.C.E.

In today's Bergama one catches sight of two images at once. One is a feeling created by the ancient city, a large part of which, including the Alter of Zeus, is exhibited in the Berlin Pergamon Museum. A kind of pride that is not easy to define. I am not able to avoid mentioning the subject of Berlin. For even if one does not blame the Western world, even if one doesn't much speak of it out loud, however you look at it, this is a matter of considerable ambivalence. The situation is diametrically opposed to the principle of exhibiting an excavated historical work in its original location, or at least as nearby as possible. This has been going on for almost a century. For those who do not know, let me say that Berlin is two thousand kilometers from Bergama. One cannot help but wonder what would have happened if the situation were reversed. If, for example, a historical work excavated in Berlin had been exhibited in Bergama all this time. Who knows what hell would have been raised. One can scarcely imagine. Just between you and me, I cannot say that this double-standard neo-colonial ambiance does not bother me. Anyway, I digress, though much more could be said.

Even in its present incomplete state, the Acropolis serving as the capitol of the Kingdom of Pergamon from the third century B.C.E. presents the physical manifestations of an urban culture constructed upon a long-established civilization. Administrative, religious, cultural, and mercantile functions came together in this settlement; as new structures were articulated side by side, they did not compromise its special orthogonal geometry, and the empty spaces remaining were used as opulent public areas. The scale of the ancient theater, huge even by today's standards, gives an idea of how rich the city's social and cultural life was. One cannot but be awed by the city's powerful structural grammar and monumental bearing.

The image projected by the new city when one looks down from the Acropolis is another story. It has become increasingly built-up in recent years, and what now stretches out below is a rural fabric that has lost its homogeneous structure. The typical low-rise configuration often seen in many regions of Turkey has begun to give way to those familiar mid-size apartment buildings. The most important element delineating the city image is the Cumhuriyet Boulevard along which stand several public buildings that may be described as works of the Republican Era. Happily, these structures have, at least for the time being, escaped the revanchist[7] trend that has in recent years gradually increased its field of activity against similar period buildings in several regions of the country. Other than two cinemas, one quite old, a small theater and a library, there is no sign of cultural life in the county worth mentioning.

So... Are these two ways of being: the Acropolis and the new city of Bergama, at first glance almost completely at odds, in any even implicit way parallel? Can an, at least notional, relationship be established between them? The more I ask myself such questions, the stranger they seem to me. I leave the city with the idea I should come up with the description of a structure that can host the cultural life of today's Bergama, rather than produce a forced short-circuit between two different cultures. And without being afraid to be influenced by the rich memory the place keeps hidden...

I am at the Istanbul office sitting around the table with the team we have put together for this job. The project site is on the main boulevard and across from a park much used by the people of Bergama. The commercial units lined up all along the Cumhuriyet Boulevard in a relatively orderly manner from the north on down toward the site intrude precisely in this undefined area to overflow indifferently onto the sidewalk. The makeshift shops continuing along three sides of the site, human in scale and random in nature, appear to be rooted in the city's memory in some way.

Now that I have seen them with my own eyes it seems even more meaningful to avoid displacing the shopkeepers and preserve the liveliness of the commercial life there.

We bring the commercial units on the Cumhuriyet Boulevard a step back and create an arcade in front of them, preserving the boulevard-long alignment. We discuss the possibility of forming a controlled interior courtyard space by maintaining this system to embrace three sides of the project site. If we have shops facing both in and out, the interior shops will invigorate the life inside the courtyard. I draw quick sketches on the whiteboard behind us as we talk. In the end, we decide to make a three-dimensional model of this idea and use it to determine exact measurements.

On another day we talk about Cultural Center structure typology. We discuss at length the concept of the "Culture Industry" with reference to Adorno and the Frankfurt School. Various opinions fly through the air about the sociability of artistic and philosophical works and their relationship, or more often lack of relationship, to everyday life. The opinion that seems to win out is that works of culture and art, or theater, will be attractive and sustainable to the degree they can accommodate everyday life or, from another point of view, mechanisms of consumption. The majority thinks there is a kind of distancing, othering, and as a result a significant loss of attraction, at the point where sophistication becomes overly dominant. Completing the dialectical analysis, I maintain that when the reverse is the case, in other words when the drive to consumption overwhelms the work so that it is shaped by that concern, there is an unavoidable loss of depth...

We place the courtyard's three blocks, the library, cinemas, and main hall, at the north end of the site. The asymmetrical spaces between them can be used as common areas.

The Çamlı Park on the other side of the boulevard has been adopted by the city's people and is an intensively used public space. It emerges as an attractive idea to take advantage of that and make it easy for the users of the park to flow into the Cultural Center. The idea is readily fleshed out by having the park six to seven meters above the level of the road. We tie the park crowd on the one hand, and a bridge passageway continuing the thick fabric of greenery over the road on the other, to the open-air cinema at the top elevation of the project and the interior foyer area at that level. We also bring the passageway down to the courtyard level by way of stairs at a soft incline. Once again I emphasize to my friends how very important permeability and relatedness to the city are for such projects. We affirm the value in having the bridge passageway significantly increase that permeability.

It is important that the arcade which running continuously along three sides of the work tie together the commercial liveliness of the two parallel boulevards as a sheltered pedestrian way.

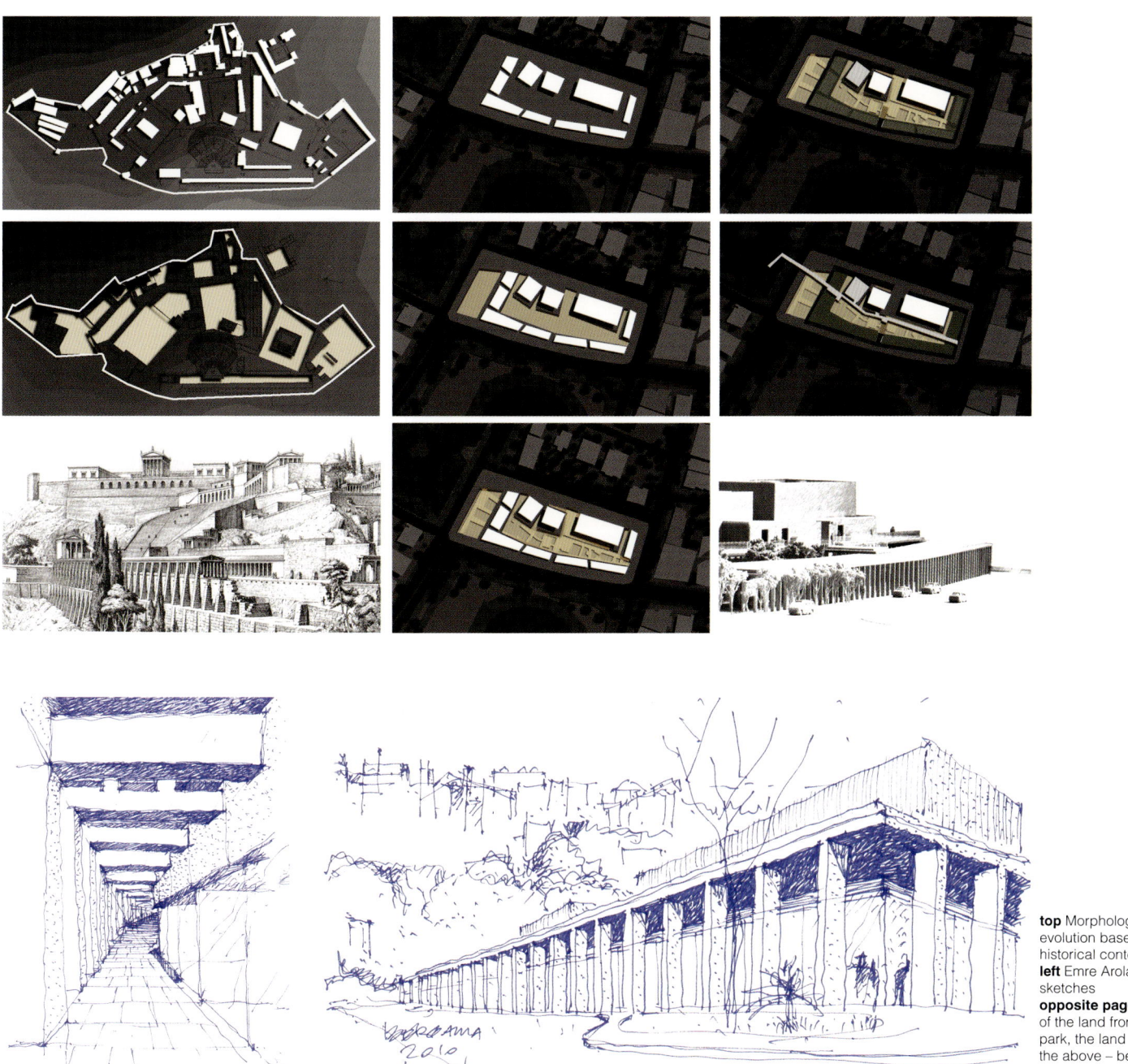

top Morphological evolution based on historical context
left Emre Arolat's sketches
opposite page View of the land from the park, the land from the above – before the construction

We also make a passageway between the two main blocks with the wall demarcating the car park. We envisage the wall becoming a kind of information and communication surface, and the passageway as an exhibition path that will also connect the two boulevards.

We did not discuss materials at all during this design process. Materials are not a subject much spoken of in our design group anyway. We have done this many times. If the design is sufficiently nuanced, and of high enough quality, the question of materials resolves itself. In other words, that subject is not really a multiple-choice matter for us. It gives itself up in the way the site whispers to you. The important thing is to know how to listen, to manage to hear and understand. It happens like that with the Bergama project too. The powerful mass construct of the work, and the rich composition it affords, lead us to a nakedness, or to put in another way, a kind of primariness, that leaves the material to withdraw as much a possible into the background. And, it is a precondition that the project had to be built on a rather low budget and require minimum upkeep. In light of these thoughts, we decide to leave the external surfaces as exposed concrete, performing a simple procedure to protect them from external factors. We envisage that the texture of the concrete, to be poured with a simple wooden mold, will give the work a tactile quality.

After working feverishly for nearly three months, we invite the Major to Istanbul in order to present to him our first thoughts and project concept. In our detailed presentation, we portray the project as a kind of culture generator that will bring the citizens of Bergama into a direct relationship with its quality spaces and potentially enrich the city's daily life.

He smiles, saying, *"This is a done deal."*

A few weeks later we present the project to a much larger group at Bergama's historical library building. We answer questions. There is a general feeling of satisfaction in the air. A small number of attendees are clearly of the political opposition. Some make odd but unimportant comments. Later the apparently fieriest of them take the floor. *"What kind of weird project is this? It reminds me of the Ancient Greek cities!"* he bursts forth in a whining shout. *"There is no national architecture here, we cannot have it!"* he continues, thinking that supports his argument. I try to halt the smile that is spreading across my face as I catch the eye of one of our team I have been working with for months. And all at once we both direct our gaze to the same hill where the ancient city looks down upon us...

The project requires approval from various official bodies before construction documents can be drawn up. *"I hope all procedures will be completed by the first months of the new year,"* says the Mayor.

The year is 2010, the month is September.

top The park, the acropolis, and the land during the construction
far left Mold assembly with textured surface timber
left Emre Arolat's site visit

I Am Not the Kind of Architect You Are Used To...

It is a few days after we return from Bergama. There are dozens of ongoing projects at the office. For years I have made an effort to set aside enough time for each project one by one. However important well-equipped teams and offices that run like clockwork are in the world of architecture today, I tend to push all things to the limit, attending tirelessly to every different issue of a project so as to be in control of every detail and produce the most attractive solution at every stage. And to do that, ease of communication is indispensable. Sometimes in order to get to the bottom of something we have to be able to talk for a whole day. I also put great importance on discussing the conversations about a project I've had with clients with my design colleagues at the office. I believe there can be something to be learned from everyone.

And I listen to him with all the attention I have. He is talking about family dinners attended by hundreds of people, about peculiar feuds between those with opposing views. We laugh. I actually know part of the family from another project. But this is the first time I've met Suat Bey.[8] He talks about the Social Aid Foundation he established and the projects he has already completed and does not suppress the gleam in his eye. He shows me photographs of hospitals, nursing homes, and a mosque completed a few years ago in Siirt.[9]

"We thought you would be the right architect for this project," he says, looking straight into my eyes. I wonder what makes him say that. I don't want him to see what I am thinking, and avert my eyes involuntarily. I ask myself if they are making a mistake. I have never built a mosque before...

Later I wonder if I was a bit rude. I didn't beat around the bush but said straightaway, *"I am not the kind of architect you are used to. Whatever your expectations may be, I will never do a project that doesn't agree with me."* He was sulking as he left the office.

In fact, one side of me is dying to do this project. The other side is not much interested. A little voice whispers that this is not a ball for me to kick. We would never build a replica classic Ottoman mosque. If we take this step, it will have to be a bold one. In any case, we would not be content to just bend the parameters of a structural typology invented centuries ago or to interpret that familiar schema. Obviously, it would be better not to do it at all.

I go to the next meeting. This time I am thinking of a photograph I saw half an hour earlier. A light of obscure source hitting the surface of a distant lake. Slightly withered vegetation in front. It is eating away at me.

I say to the colleagues I plan to work with on the design team, *"There is no doubt that much can be learned from the essence of schemas repeated for centuries. But in my opinion no one needs another version of that 500-year-old model. It is meaningless to work that way. Let us do what we know to be right."*

left Mosque in Siirt
below View from the land towards the lake

top Suleymaniye Mosque of Sinan sketched by Emre Arolat
above Sheikh Zayed Mosque in Abu Dhabi is among the landmarks of Islamic Architecture, known as one of the most expensive buildings of the world sketched by Emre Arolat

"And let's not overthink the rest. There is no law saying we have to build everything we design, for that matter. It is quite possible that this will not be built either. Even if the project to be produced is like a dream, still I can see it before my eyes. It will not be easy to accept or to get it accepted. We can be sure of that. That is the fate of certain projects. If you like, we can even approach this design as a kind of academic workshop in Islamic architecture. At the very worst, the theoretical framework we set forth will serve as the source of a publication. The President of the Foundation called again today. He conveyed his determination to have us do this together. I reiterated my concerns about his expectations. He said a few words about how he could be open to new ideas, and now he has given us enough time to do the design. Certainly, there is no guarantee here. But I have the feeling we should do it. So let's take this project all the way, without compromise."

I look into their eyes one by one. They seem convinced. Then I turn to Gonca.[10] She is wagging her head wryly. We all know very well that there will be no material gain from this project that the Social Aid Foundation has put before us. It is perfectly clear that it will be financed by our office. She shrugs her shoulders. *"What good would it do for me to object?"* Then she turns to the work before her, mumbling, *"You won't listen anyway..."*

It is obvious that this job will not be easy. First of all, we make up a reading list. Nil[11] copies texts she thinks important and sends them to me, texts from Oleg Grabar to Mohammed Arkoun, from Hossein Nasr to Fatema Mernissi, even going back to the likes of al-Ghazzal and Ibn Rushd. And, of course the Koran itself. Now to read the Turkish paraphrases once again.

I can say that I have long had a serious interest in Islamic philosophy anyway. Since the subject has come up, let me confess that I have a view I haven't much shared with anyone yet that the undiluted, spiritual side of that philosophy, when combined with updated positivist principles purged of fanaticism, might be transformed into a phenomenon capable of overcoming savage capitalism. But to design a mosque is another matter. Especially if you bring new customs to the old village...

For the first few weeks, we just read, research, and share our thoughts with one another. I have always found this process important. Some architects draw in order to think, but I find it right to think long and hard, to discuss and analyze, before starting any kind of drawing. I often recommend this way of going about things to my design colleagues at the office, and to my students. Think first, then draw, instead of thinking while drawing...

I get together with the design team almost every other day. It is important to be tight in the first stage. While some tendencies that emerge in this first period lose their importance, others get stronger all during the intellectual production process and can become indispensable principles. And so it happens this time. As a result of a period of intense discussion, a shared vision is adopted by which the work to be designed will be purged of historical cultural burdens as much as possible and thus a direct, pure emotionality of the essence of worship brought to the fore. With that in mind, as we have done so often before, we examine once again the most ancient examples and archetypes of such works. And we see that neither in the Koran nor in any other source to be taken seriously is there any physical description concerning a mosque. Moreover, we once more encounter the truth that every place on earth can be a place of worship. There is only one condition, that it be clean...

It takes us more than two months to get to the point where we feel comfortable about the project. I call Suat Bey about giving a pre-presentation. I want to first present the design before a group limited to a few people including himself. I am not much hopeful, but still, I think I might get lucky and this way could convince them, that is, convince the less conservative part of the family. As for the rest, we will think that out with them.

"They are here," says my assistant, looking at me anxiously. Before I can speak she goes on excitedly, *"You said a few people were coming but there are at least twenty people downstairs. I hear that one of them is the Mufti of Büyükçekmece.[12] I showed everyone into the large auditorium."*

I take a deep breath and try to calm myself. I recall what I told my friends two months earlier when I had just begun to work on this project. Yes, we did what we thought was right. And we took our idea as far as it would go. It had been a high quality, productive process. The fact is I am happy about having come as far as we have. The rest is up to them...

They watch the images on the screen in rapt attention. I carry on giving my speech while I look at each of them in the eye. At that point I see Leyla[13] sitting in one of the back rows. She is clearly very excited. In fact, she has worked very hard on this project as one of the youngest members of the design team. No visual indicating what the work will look like has been shown yet. So far I have been speaking more about general topics and the purity and humility at the essence of Islamic philosophy. I am saying that it is one of the influences on early Islamic architecture and that the pretentiousness, the love of empty show so often seen in the geography of Islam in recent years is something quite the reverse. A frozen expression of indecision reigns on the faces of the spectators illuminated by the projector. I think that the moment of truth will come later when after all this talk they see what the work will actually look like.

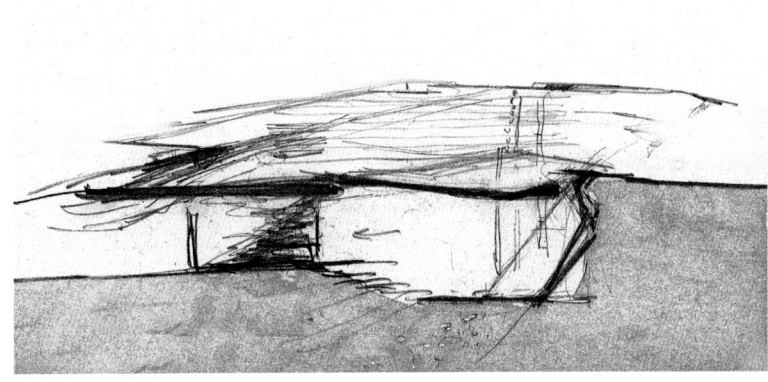

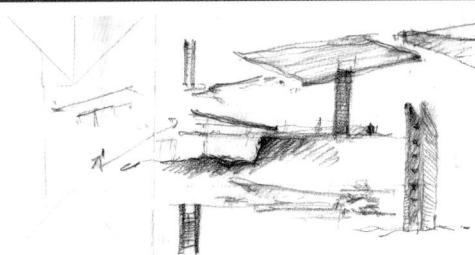

top First sketch by Emre Arolat, November 2010
above Sketch by Emre Arolat, December 2010
left Sketch by Emre Arolat, January 2011
bottom left Sketch for the wall textures by Emre Arolat, January 2011
bottom right Sketch for cascades by Emre Arolat, January 2011

"It is precisely here that the work settles gradually into the natural slope of the site, as you can see. It does not disrupt and transform its surroundings. On the contrary, it almost shares the mood of its surroundings. It does not shout for our attention as many works do. It is happy to be where it is, as if it has always been there. It is as if some people or others have been worshipping there for centuries. A space of calm meets us as we approach the upper courtyard. This is the upper courtyard. It opens onto the lake from the other direction. We reach the entrance by going down the cascade staircase, which is determined by the slope of the site."

"When we enter the space inside is also calm and quiet. There are no divisions or load-bearing elements. A few steps leading down to the prayer niche wall amplify the depth of the space. During worship, these steps may also be used as prayer spaces. The elderly or those with physical disabilities could do their prayers seated there."

"The dome is a feature that emerged centuries ago as a simple practical covering for the space. It does not, as many suppose it does, have any direct connection with Islamic architecture or Sufism. It is apparently a structural technique developed so as to be able to cover a square total space without the use of pillars. Today we use completely different techniques to cover spaces. Thus, it did not seem meaningful to us in this project to reproduce the dome purely as a form because we are used to it. We propose to take advantage of new techniques instead."

"For example, the form of the ceiling in the main worship hall is determined by the reflection in the inner space of the topographical composition formed by the vegetation on top of it. This lightens the weight of the reinforced concrete covering's central section. And I want particularly to emphasize that we are not offering a new house of worship typology with this work. This work is designed for this and only this particular site. In other words, it is not a design that could be reproduced elsewhere. The truth is I do not much like facile categorizations of typology, whatever the subject at hand. We can say that this is more a modernist and contextual approach. In addition, it has a quite original primariness in its constitution. The real reason we used almost no materials other than exposed concrete and natural stone was to achieve this. The work's sole ornament is the natural light that will lick the prayer niche wall, changing color as the day goes on."

A gradually increasing murmur rises from one corner of the auditorium. A few people talking among themselves realize others are listening to them and quiet down. It is clear from the expression on their faces that they are not at all pleased by the design or my presentation of it.

"Now I must tell you about the women's section," I say, continuing. Now whatever will be, will be. I sense that I have long passed the point of caring what anyone will say, and I continue with abandon. "For here too, we propose an unusual approach. Women will be able to worship right next to men, in the very first row, only a few steps higher in an area reserved for themselves. A simple screen will break the direct visual connection in between."

The eyes of the audience are becoming duller and duller. My colleagues have turned up the lights now that the presentation is over. It is as if no one wants to be the first to speak. No one makes a sound. Gradually all eyes turn toward the Mufti. He is wearing a gray-green suit. He begins to speak, glancing at Suat Bey.

"The truth is, it is a very interesting project. Our architect has explained his thinking in detail. If I had not heard this, I might have thought the design very strange. But now I am thinking, why not? It seems to me that it might really fit that place."

Someone in the group from which the murmuring arose earlier immediately objects. He says that this mosque doesn't look like a mosque, and in fact doesn't look like anything at all. A few people next to him nod in approval. Now there are three differing opinions in the auditorium. Those who are completely against it, those who can't decide, and those who believe, although the design doesn't seem quite right to them, that it could be tried. The debate goes on. Now and then everyone agrees on something. I prefer to say nothing and simply watch. It is clear no one wants to hear my opinion at this point anyway. I have said enough. The Mufti of Büyükçemece again has the last word. This time he looks directly at me.

"This is a very unusual project. As I said earlier, speaking for myself, it is all right with me. But I do not think I can decide this by myself. As you can see, even members of the family, several of them, do not favor it. If it were the sort of mosque we are used to, it would have been much easier. But things being what they are, we will have to present it to the Mufti of Istanbul and get his approval."

A few weeks later we are in the Istanbul Mufti's office. This time there are only three of us, Suat Bey, Nil, and me. I have looked into the man a bit. He is the Professor of Divinity Mustafa Bey, and he has published hundreds of articles.[14] He greets us politely.

We talk about this and that for a short while and then I make the same presentation for him. I mention contemporary issues of Islamic societies and how they affect contemporary trends in Islamic architecture, and in that context, I set forth the conceptual framework in which the project places itself. He often nods his head in approval of what I am saying. He interrupts to ask a brief question now and then. It is clear that he takes both this project and what I am saying very seriously.

above left The reflection of the exterior topography becomes a sophisticated articulation on the ceiling of the main hall
above The light on the Quiblah wall, construction photograph
left The slit and the light washing the Quiblah wall, sketch by Emre Arolat, February 2011

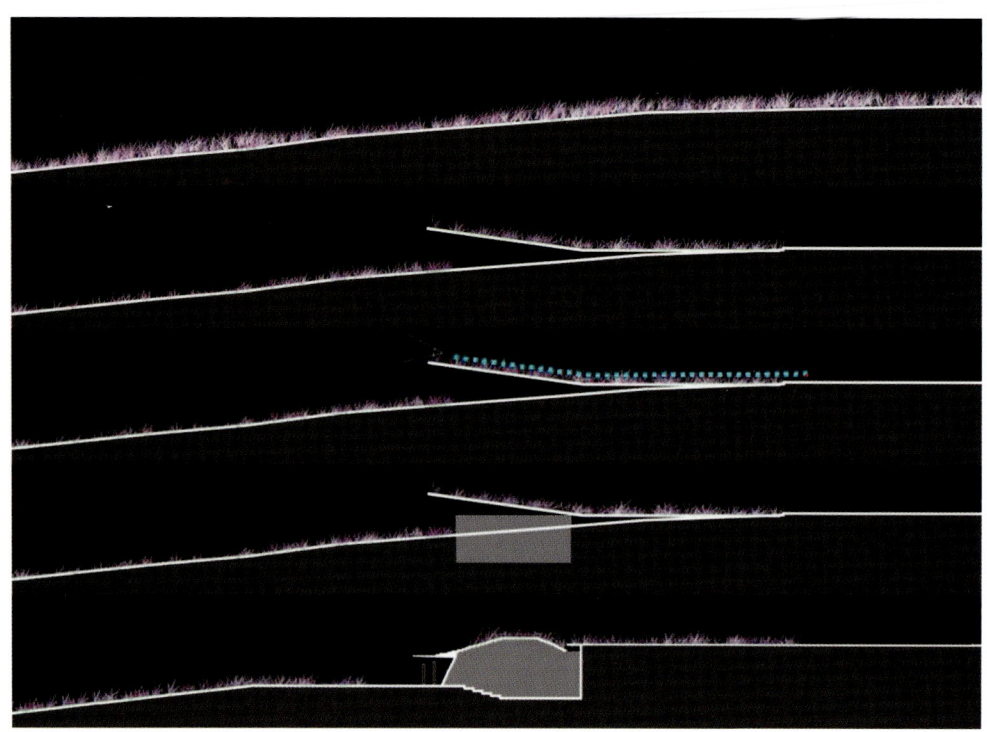

left Sections indicating the gentle interference with the topography
bottom Sketch by Emre Arolat, February 2011
opposite page Woman praying at the forefront

The presentation takes more than an hour. I thank him for listening to me for so long. He is quiet at first, a slight smile on his face. Then he takes a deep breath and pronounces that sentence I will probably never forget all my life.

"Suat Bey, I want to pray in this mosque as soon as possible."

There is a brief silence. Suat Bey is pleased. His eyes are laughing. I am caught between surprise and joy. We both know that this sentence is tantamount to permission to build Sancaklar Mosque. Mustafa Bey continues.

"I really do like this project very much. In recent years mosque architecture has painted itself into a corner, and I believe this design has the power to bring a breath of fresh air to the matter. Even worldwide. But the thesis the project puts forth, and thus also your approach to it, is as important is the project itself. What you say about the relationship between religion and morality, in particular, is really on the mark. Unfortunately even a large number of those who call themselves scholars of Islam do not understand the moral backbone that takes the central place in the totality of our faith. The watchword of humility you mentioned earlier in your presentation is, in fact, all bound up with this. Unfortunately, the Islam that takes a character as its central principle has been abandoned and a legalistic Islam emptied of moral essence has taken its place."

The year is 2011, the month is February.

The Thing Called a Marina...

Bodrum, or as it was known in ancient times, Halicarnassus. A place unique onto itself, the cradle of many civilizations from the Dorians to the Carians, the Byzantines to the Ottomans. And at the same time, with its head-spinning transformation over the past 40-50 years, one of the most conspicuous footprints of Turkey's socio-cultural changes. From a lovably shabby, authentic little seaside town to a chaotic, mixed-up settlement area flung all across the shores of a giant peninsula. Growing fast and less distinctive the bigger it gets.

Site of the countless wild adventures of my high school years in pursuit of a lover who often drove me out of my mind. I would be seized by longing for her and suddenly decide to leap up and go after her. On the road, I would listen to the same singer with the burning voice sing the same songs on the car cassette player and then wait for the bright orange sun of the morning to rise at cheap pensions with black scorpions scurrying up their whitewashed walls. Never sleeping. Unfortunately, people grow up...

I first saw Mübariz Mansimov[15] at one of the gala evenings organized by Istanbul Modern.[16] That day he had paid a very high price to buy the most expensive work auctioned off for the benefit of various educational institutions. One of my friends at the table says he is an Azeri shipping magnate. He later gradually became better known in Turkey. One day I read in the newspaper that he had bought the Yalıkavak Marina in Bodrum. I met the young man a few weeks later when a mutual friend introduced us.

You know how you can sense a person's intelligence from the gleam in their eye, well Mübariz Bey is a good example of that. He talks with great enthusiasm about his ideas for the new marina he wants to build. He speaks surprisingly good Turkish. *"We are going to tear down the old marina buildings completely. You and I have to build the world's most beautiful marina here."* I like men with big dreams like that. The truth is, that childish excitement of his is impressive and he is not at all shy about letting it show.

A few months later, we are at the office of the Palmali Companies Group to give a presentation on the first phase of design. All around us are carefully arranged glass cupboards filled with hundreds of machines and parts having to do with overseas shipping. I gaze in amazement at these shiny brass pieces made for I don't know what purpose. Many photographs of ships on the walls. Gigantic steamers.

I have given presentations to hundreds of clients, all unlike one another, in many different places in the world. A vast herd of people, some deeply interested in art and architecture and some not at all. Among them, heads of state, prime ministers, academicians with big egos, intellectuals sharp as whips, bored bureaucrats, and some who tried to hide their sense of inferiority behind the arrogance come of earning a great deal of money all of a sudden. But I am as jumpy inside as if it were my first time. I am like that almost every time I give a presentation. I have a huge knot inside my belly.

The long-legged Russian secretary accompanies us as far as the meeting room where we will give the presentation. The place is packed. Clearly, they have gathered some time earlier. There are at least twenty people sitting around a long table. A few faces are familiar. It will take a long time now to shake the hand of each one...

The knot in my belly melts away as soon as I begin. Now it is as if I am the most self-confident man in the world. That is the good part of this life. It is always that way. I generally calculate the length of a presentation according to the feeling I get from the audience. The people here seem very different to the other, so it will be a good thing to keep it on the short side. And not theorize much. If they cannot understand, they will get bored. If that happens, they will start chattering and my presentation will fall flat.

"The specific characteristics of the site have always been the input most important to us," I begin. One of the most important issues is to keep in view how financially unsuccessful the existing marina has been. It is hoped that the new situation will turn this around. The only medicine for it is to increase the number of functions here and thus the number of users. And in order to achieve that, the marina must be purged of its familiar elitist restrictiveness. That is the fundamental problem because it requires a kind of paradigm shift. Now, let's see you come and explain that to the local big shots around the table.

"It is difficult for marinas to become public spaces in the true sense because their number of users is limited. For the same reason, they do not attract crowds. This is a situation that a great majority of boat owners, in fact, prefer, though they may not say so. They find this kind of social distance convenient in the context of their own class belonging. And they connect these arguments to the issue of security as well. The truth is, I see this as a fear derived from a self-fulfilling prophecy. Perhaps this is the first issue we should address while drawing up the project. If true financial success is a goal, the marina must become the most important center of attraction in the region. The only way to achieve that is to come up with a plan for the venue that brings different socio-economic classes together. For we are talking about a large site of 100,000 square meters. This is not an area size that can be brought to life without spaces that can be used by the middle class. Thus for this project, we have to wipe out the image that first comes to mind when we hear the word 'marina,' and create a unique place that can be used by the masses."

top Bodrum in 1948
above Bodrum in 2018

I find the social vein of the architecture profession and its potential for discovering solutions to social problems by way of quality design very important. Over the years I have grasped that there can be grounds for appreciating this either directly, or in a less obvious way. Sometimes you get a job where the benefit to the public is right there in front of you. The Bergama Cultural Center and the Sancaklar Mosque for example, which I mentioned before, were just such projects. In both projects economic gain was secondary. At other times you as the architect can bring to light a public good or potential for public space that is not apparent at first glance. That is the case with the Yalıkavak Marina project. But it is obvious that now, even if I come out shouting about how there is a great potential for the public good here, no one will notice it because that kind of basic human element is simply not visible in the neoliberal world in which we now live. Such concepts as sensitivity to the natural environment, human scale, human design, public good, and public space do not create social enthusiasm. Forget creating enthusiasm, such things can be regarded as the definition of defeatist or anarchist fantasies. Eyes, ears, and minds open only when you put before them concepts like an economic model, productivity or profitability. I continue talking, my mind on these realities.

"Yes, this project must attract to itself not merely five or six hundred boat owners but tens of thousands of users living in or visiting the region as tourists. It must become a center, an attractive destination that also houses a marina. Thus in the planning stage, we came up with a solution that is as permeable and fluid as possible. We can be certain that some boat owners will not like seeing the destruction of the peaceful atmosphere to which they are accustomed. There will be at least ten times the number of people there are now walking around the site. You will sometimes even hear complaints about noise. We have to take that on. Now and then some excesses may occur that will annoy you as well. It is very important that all that should melt away in the density of people and the allure of the site. Crowds and the dense parts of cities have that power, an allure that cannot be resisted. We must use that."

The images I have projected on the screen have not yet included any design object. My intention is rather to prepare the theoretical ground for the design I will shortly put forth. I find this kind of preamble important in order to mentally prepare the audience before putting forth a shocking proposal. But still, it should not go on too long. Now, little by little, the time is coming for the three-dimensional visual we have painstakingly prepared.

"Another goal of my design was to create the architectural equivalent of the basic idea I tried to explain to you earlier, and have the allure I mentioned come alive in flesh and blood. Yes, there is no doubt whatsoever that the works to be placed here must provide every imaginable functional need without exception. We must make it the best-equipped marina in the Mediterranean. But at the same time, the design must use a language that can engage in dialogue with the specific characteristics of the place. The structures you see form a precisely Mediterranean succession of spaces. But such contextual approaches are extremely critical. If you get carried away, you may fall into the trap of folkloric form. Bodrum is filled with the kitschiest examples of that. On the other hand, at the other extreme, there is the risk of a mediocrity that might be overly generic. These structures are of different sizes and heights according to function and need, and have been composed in a singular form. What you see at the left of the screen is the settlement of Ancient Miletus. On the right is our proposal for the first stage of the marina. Actually, the entire planning follows an implied grid layout that does not catch the eye at first glance. These fragments formed by the covered, open, or partially covered spaces of varied eating-drinking units face a long wall that is sometimes a dividing and sometimes permeable element."

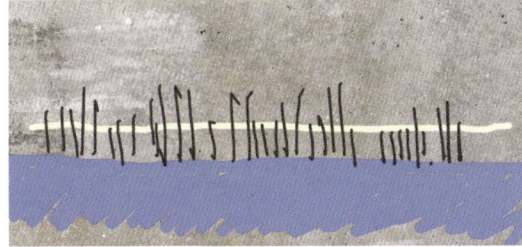

left A horizontal line behind the poles, sketch by Emre Arolat
below Infinity pool, sketch by Emre Arolat
opposite page Texture, sketch by Emre Arolat

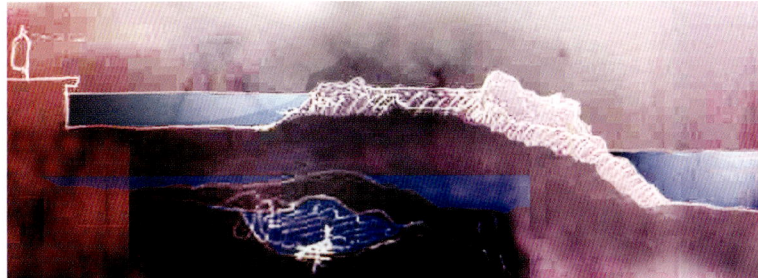

"*Now for the material and texture relationships. Just as in so many ancient Mediterranean cities, here too the surfaces of works and roads are defined with one material. Travertine-based natural stone in a few different tones will with the rough structure of its surface protect the works from the effects of sun and sea year in year out. On the other hand, I think this approach will create a kind of sense of timelessness in the whole of the work. Thus the structures will not be alienated from the geography on which they stand. But neither will they behave like replicas. In sum, our fundamental goal here is a design approach both reminiscent of certain places and also new and fresh...*"

After these sentences I have the animation that puts forth various scenarios for the use of the space started and, as always, look carefully at their faces. Everyone seems surprisingly pleased. I watch the smiles spreading on some faces as the film goes on. Afterwards, there is a short silence. I answer a few questions. Whenever this many people get together, there will definitely be a few who like to talk about architecture and put forth their views. Architecture is a profession by nature quite open to critique and varying opinions. People with some connection to architecture can with surprising ease offer strange interpretations of something you have arrived at after a thousand and one kinds of analysis and months of painstaking work. After all, it is not heart surgery we are talking about. In other words, it is not like suggesting that we tie off that vein a little higher up. As they say, everyone who has a mouth talks.

A few moments later Mübariz Bey takes the floor. Clearly, his patience has been sorely tried. And he is doing the brief talk closing the session.

"*Alright now, let's forget that for now. It's a good project. It suits my way of thinking very well. We will begin construction immediately. Everyone should be prepared. Tomorrow we are in Bodrum...*"

The year is 2011, the month is July.

above Lighthouse, sketch by Emre Arolat
right Peninsula, sketch by Emre Arolat
opposite page Travertine, the main material as a timeless approach

Conclusion

Construction of the Bergama Cultural Center began in 2011, after preparation of the application projects and the tender bidding. A while later, in a stroke of bad luck, the owner of the construction company died and in 2014 work was halted before completion of the basic fabrication. The municipality organized a new tender for the rest of the work. A new construction company took over after a year and a half, and it was opened for use at the end of 2016.

Construction of Sancaklar Mosque and Yalıkavak Marina, both private sector works, moved much more quickly. The Mosque was finished at the end of 2013, and the Marina, the following year. Although these three projects, which came up at the same time and were parallel in respect of design and period of construction, do not at first glance much resemble one another, I believe they have several shared characteristics. Briefly, I can say that these works, like most others we have done, were designed with an architectural view that relies upon specific context and situation. And all three are products of a kind of common design tendency that tests the limits of habitual usage and blurs the boundaries of understanding in the environments where they are placed.

In this piece, I have tried, as a member of the team that designed these works to relate my experiences, opinions, and thoughts concerning all three as honestly and directly as possible. My views are without a doubt, for the most part, personal and because they are personal, subjective. It could even be claimed that in that sense they are quite speculative. All three works have been in use for a while and open to the public. It pleases me greatly that they are used very much. The people of Bergama love the Cultural Center and have taken it as their own. Sancaklar Mosque has a loyal congregation. And it has thousands of visitors from all over the world who are interested in architecture. The Yalıkavak Marina is so popular that it has transformed its entire surroundings. Who knows, perhaps some of those who read this piece will later view those works and see the stories I have told come alive before their eyes. There is no doubt that a great majority will understand them through their own experiences. Maybe some will love them and others will hate them. Some will adopt them and visit them often, while others will never set foot in them again.

How could it be otherwise anyway?

above A design review in EAA Istanbul office
opposite page in order
Bergama Cultural Center, after completion
Sancaklar Mosque, after completion
Yalikavak Marina, after completion

Notes

[1] Etiler is a neighborhood in Istanbul's Beşiktaş district. The offices of EAA-Emre Arolat Architecture were active there 2005-2010.

[2] *Radikal* was a social liberal daily newspaper published by the Dogan Holding Media Group 1996-2014.

[3] The Aga Khan Award for Architecture is a prize awarded once every three years to projects that set new world standards of excellence in architecture, planning practices, historic preservation and landscape architecture.

[4] Mehmet Gönenç, Mayor of Bergama Municipality, was born in Bergama in 1970. He graduated from the Department of Public Administration in the Istanbul University Faculty of Political Science in 1994. In 2009, running as the Republican People's Party candidate, he was elected Mayor of Bergama Municipality. He again ran as candidate of the same party in 2014 and was re-elected to the same post.

[5] Prof. Dr. Murat Güvenç is an academician who received his B.A. and M.A. from Middle East Technical University's Faculty of Architecture City and Regional Planning Department. He did work on issues of Ankara Greater Municipality planning, city modeling, industrial region theory and the industrial geography of Istanbul, publishing many articles. Since 2014 he has been a member of the faculty at the Political Science and Public Administration Science Department of Kadir Has University, and also serves as Director of the Istanbul Studies Center.

[6] METU, Middle East Technical University, Ankara, Turkey.

[7] The revanchist trend is a kind of conservative or conservatising movement put forth by the regime in many areas in recent years. It aims to erase the traces of the cultural turn the Republic created by placing incentives to Westernization at its center. Within the framework of this movement many modernist buildings symbolizing the Republican Era have been torn down, and an architectural tendency we may call "Neo-Ottomanist," having no intellectual infrastructure whatsoever, has been brought to the fore.

[8] Suat Sancak, Deputy Chairman of the Sancak Group Board of Directors and President of the Sancaklar Foundation for Education, Health, Culture and Social Aid.

[9] Siirt, A province in southeastern Turkey, and the place where the Sancak family originated.

[10] Gonca Paşolar, Architect, co-founder and managing partner, EAA-Emre Arolat Architecture.

[11] Nil Aynalı Eğler, Architect, worked at EAA-Emre Arolat Architecture 2010-2014.

[12] Mehmet Narin occupied the office of Mufti of Büyükçekmece during the time Sancaklar Mosque was being built. In Turkey a mufti is a government official who oversees the religious affairs of a province or county.

[13] Leyla Kori, Architect, She has worked at the EAA-Emre Arolat Architecture office since 2008. She was among the architects on the design team during the Sancaklar Mosque project. Today she works at EAA as a Project Group Leader.

[14] Prof. Dr. Mustafa Çağrıcı is the academic who occupied the office of Istanbul Mufti while Sncaklar Mosque was being built.

[15] Mübariz Mansimov is a Turkish businessman of Azeri extraction. He owns many national and international groups of companies active in sectors such as tourism administration, shipping, and construction.

[16] Istanbul Modern is Turkey's first modern art museum. It was founded by the Istanbul Foundation for Culture and the Arts at the initiative of the Eczacıbaşı family and opened in 2004.

Bergama Cultural Center
İzmir

Sancaklar Mosque
İstanbul

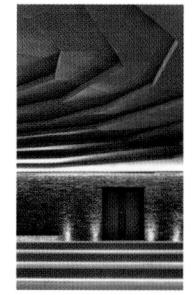

Yalıkavak Marina
Bodrum

Project Credits

Bergama Cultural Center
İzmir, Turkey
2013 - 16
Client: Bergama Municipality
Project Architects: Rıfat Yılmaz
Team: Aylin Yılmaz, Anıl Biçer, Fatih Tezman, Can Dinçer, Neslihan Avşarlıgil, Ayça Yontarım, İdris Ayar, Taner Arıkan, Nurgül Yardım, İpek Baycan, Ercan Yılmaz, Selin Gündüz, Ulya Köseoğlu, Deniz Kösemen, Emre Tunay
Contractor: Gürsel Ltd. & Ümsan Ltd JV, Magnesia Ltd.
Structural Engineer: Nodus Engineering Consulting Co.
Services Engineers: Beta Technic, Aykar Engineering
Lighting Consultant: Tepta Lighting
Façade Consultant: Axis Facades
Landscape Design: DS Architects
Acoustic: Sey Consulting
Stage Consultant: Anne Minors Performance Consultants, Sound Space Vision-Theatre Planning & Acoustics
Signage: Başak Atalay Design Studio
Awards:
2017 The Plan Award, "Completed Culture," Finalist
2017 Blueprint Awards, "Best Public-Use Project with Public Funding," Finalist
2017 AAP - American Architecture Prize, "Architectural Design," Honorable Mention

Sancaklar Mosque
İstanbul, Turkey
2011 - 13
Client: Sancaklar Foundation
Project Architects: Nil Aynali, Leyla Kori, Uygar Yüksel
Team: Fatih Tezman, Nurdan Gürlesin, Deniz Kösemen, Ayça Yontarım, Ayşegül Taşkın, Cem Şahin, Gönül Karahan, Oya Eskin Güvendi, Taha Alkan, Ünal Ali Özger
Contractor: Sancaklar Foundation
Structural Engineer: Balkar Engineering
Services Engineers: Setta Engineering, HB Technic
Lighting Consultant: SLD – Piero Castiglioni
Landscape Design: EAA-Emre Arolat Architecture, Modesa, DS Architects
Acoustic: Sey Consulting
Artwork: Mehmed Özçay (calligraphy)
Awards:
2018 RIBA International Prize for Excellence
2017 AAP - American Architecture Prize, "Misc.Architecture," Category Winner
2016 German Design Award, Excellent Communications Design Architecture
2016 World Architecture Award 23rd Cycle "Realised," "Mosques," Category Winner
2016 Bucharest Triennale, East Centric Awards, Special Award of Architext Review
2016 AICA India, "Cultural and Community Spaces," Category Winner
2015 EU Prize for Contemporary Architecture-Mies Van der Rohe Award 2015
2015 50th Zagreb Salon of Architecture Winner
2015 2A Asia Architecture Award, "Public Category," Winner
2015 Archdaily, "Religious Building of the Year," Winner
2015 Design Museum London, Designs of the Year 2015, Finalist
2015 Archmarathon 2015, "Religious Buildings," Category Winner
2015 International Award Architecture in Stone 2015, Winner
2014 XIV. National Architecture Awards, "Building Category," Winner
2013 WAF (World Architecture Festival), "Completed Buildings-Religion," Category Winner

Yalıkavak Marina
Bodrum, Turkey
2015 - 16
Client: Palmali Group
Project Architects: Rıfat Yılmaz, Leyla Kori
Team: Deniz Kösemen, Anıl Biçer, Makbule Yıldırım, Buket Kati, Bennu Tunç, Yadigar Esen
Contractor: Summa Construction, Pal Construction
Structural Engineer: Nodus Engineering Consulting Co.
Services Engineers: Beta Technic, Aykar Engineering, Deniz Project, EMT
Marine Structures: MSD
Lighting Consultant: SLD – Piero Castiglioni
Façade Consultant: Çuhadaroğlu Aluminium
Landscape Design: Çağdas Landscape, Gül Landscape
Acoustic: Sey Consulting
Infrastructure: Ekiz Project
Awards:
2017 AAP - American Architecture Prize, "Recreational Architecture," Category Winner
2016 World Architecture Award 23rd Cycle "Realised," "Tourism Buildings Other," Category Winner
2014 WAF (World Architecture Festival), "Completed Buildings-Shopping," Category Winner

Photo Credits

Bergama Municipality 33 (top)

Cemal Emden 5, 6 (top), 9 (bottom), 23 (top left, top right), 33 (bottom), 38, 41, 46 – 53, 56 – 58, 61 (all third row / all fourth row / all fifth row), 64, 67 – 72, 84 – 86, 88 (first row first, second / third row first, fourth, fifth / fourth row first, third), 89 (second row second, third / third row first, second, fourth / fourth row all), 92 – 99, 102, 106 – 117 (all), 120, 123 (bottom)

Mustafa Apan 11 (middle center, bottom), 12 (all)

Palmali Group 30, 100, 103, 104

Sancaklar Foundation 19 (top)

Studio Majo 9 (top), 43, 54, 55, 60 (bottom right), 61 (all first row / all second row)

St. Regis Istanbul 6 (bottom)

Thomas Mayer 33 (middle), 36, 39, 40, 42, 44, 60 (all except bottom right), 66, 73, 74, 76 - 83, 88 (first row third / second row all / third row second, third / fourth row second, fourth / fifth row all), 89 (first row all / second row first / third row third / fifth row all)

All other images by EAA - Emre Arolat Architecture

Authors

Aaron Betsky

Aaron Betsky is President of the School of Architecture at Taliesin. A critic of art, architecture, and design, Mr. Betsky is the author of over a dozen books on those subjects, including a forthcoming survey of modernism in architecture and design. He writes a twice-weekly blog for architectmagazine.com, 'Beyond Buildings.' Trained as an architect and in the humanities at Yale University, Mr. Betsky was previously Director of the Cincinnati Art Museum (2006-2014) and the Netherlands Architecture Institute (2001-2006), as well as Curator of Architecture and Design at the San Francisco Museum of Modern Art (1995-2001). In 2008, he also directed the 11th Venice International Biennale of Architecture. His latest books, *Making It Modern* and *Architecture Matters*, were published last year.

Emre Arolat

M. Arch., Hon. FAIA, RIBA
Founding Partner & Principal

Born in Ankara, Turkey, Emre Arolat comes from a long family tradition of architects. After graduating from Mimar Sinan Fine Arts University in Istanbul, Emre joined his parent's architecture firm Arolat Architecture, and in 2004, formed his own firm EAA - Emre Arolat Architecture with co-founder Gonca Pasolar.

Since the beginning of his architectural career, Emre Arolat has created an extraordinary body of work combining intellectual and artistic sensitivity and designing buildings large and small, tempered by the tradition and culture from which they spring. Emre's projects are largely driven by the relationship between the built and natural environment, the local culture, and invaluable knowledge and experience combined with his intuitive approach.

Emre received international recognition early on in his career, with the selected work for EU Prize for Contemporary Architecture-Mies Van der Rohe Award with the Minicity Theme Park in Antalya, Turkey (2004), and the Aga Khan Award for Architecture with the design for the Ipekyol Textile Factory in Edirne, Turkey (2006). More recently, in 2018, his Sancaklar Mosque was awarded with RIBA International Prize.

Along with his architecture practice, Emre Arolat has held a professorship at the International Academy of Architecture and is frequently invited to serve on high-profile juries, and to visiting professorships at various prominent universities and academic institutions worldwide such as the RIBA in London, the Architecture League of New York, the Pratt Institute, the Berlage Center for Advanced Studies in Architecture and Urban Design at TU-Delft in Netherlands and the Cooper Union. Recently, Emre was the Norman R. Foster Visiting Professor at the Yale School of Architecture. In 2019, Emre Arolat has been elected as an Honorary Fellow of the American Institute of Architects.

Emre Arolat has collaborated on many projects with fine arts institutions, a notable example being his collaboration with the Istanbul Foundation for Culture and Arts (IKSV), in which he worked with the organization to co-curate the first Istanbul Design Biennale.

Arolat's wide-ranging repertoire includes Zorlu Center in Istanbul, a mixed use project that serves the public with a large extensive green roof and a great plaza (2007-2014), the Antakya Museum Hotel, built above an existing archeological site in Antakya (2014-2019); the SantralIstanbul Contemporary Art Museum, the conversion and adaptive reuse of the old Ottoman Electrical Power Plant into a modern art museum (2005-2006); and the Dalaman International Airport (1999-2006), among many others.

About
EAA - Emre Arolat Architecture

EAA-Emre Arolat Architecture was established in 2004 by Emre Arolat and Gonca Pasolar in Istanbul. The practice has since expanded and now also operates from New York (2017) and London (2014).

Since its establishment in 2004, EAA has completed over 200 projects across Europe, Asia, Middle East, United Kingdom, and North America.

The practice employs about a 100 people team; architects together with a further support staff including 3D visualization artists, model makers, archivers, with administrative and secretarial staff. EAA's staff has wide experience in working with multi-disciplinary teams on building projects all over the world.

Currently, among the main projects in progress are; the Istanbul Museum of Painting and Sculpture in Istanbul, Turkey; the Reading Residential Complex in Reading, UK; the Nora Mosque and Community Center in Ajman, UAE; the METU Research Park in Ankara, Turkey.

Major projects already completed include: the Zorlu Center in Istanbul; the Sancaklar Mosque in Istanbul, the Museum Hotel Antakya in Antakya; the Abdullah Gul Presidential Museum and Library in Kayseri; the SantralIstanbul Contemporary Arts Museum in Istanbul; the Ipekyol Textile Factory in Edirne; the Mecidiyekoy Towers and Istanbul Liquor Factory in Istanbul, the Maslak No.1 Office Tower in Istanbul; the Dalaman International Airport Terminal in Mugla; the RDKM Cultural Center in Yalova; the Renovation of Entrepot Royal in Brussels and others throughout the world.

EAA's works have been displayed in institutions and exhibitions worldwide, including the Design Museum London; Royal Academy of Arts London; RIBA London; the Venice International Biennale of Architecture, Italy; the Sarajevo Green Design Festival in Sarajevo and the Prague Architecture Week in Prague.

EAA has published a compilation of its latest works in *Context and Plurality* with Rizzoli New York in 2014, the sequel, *Global and Local/ New Projects/EAA-Emre Arolat Architecture* will be published in Spring 2020, with Rizzoli Electa.

The outstanding quality of EAA's work has been recognized through awards granted by organizations such as the Royal Institute of British Architects (RIBA), the Aga Khan Foundation (AKDN), the European Union Prize for Contemporary Architecture-Mies Van der Rohe Award and the Design Museum in London.

The emphasis at EAA is on the "context", to ensure, from the start, that the design is driven by the relationship between the built and natural environment, the local culture and its specificities. Every project is approached as a new challenge with its own individual needs. In this respect, a multilayered effort at reading, researching, and understanding is undertaken in order to reveal the collective and psychological characteristics of the design.

Of course, this at the same time is a reading that includes social, economic, and ideological factors. In an architecture studio setting with production at different scales and topics, it is important to identify the specific questions of each project and individual situation, to analyze special conditions and to search for responses with an in-depth understanding of the given situation.

EAA works closely with acclaimed consultants and also with the clients to establish an integrated design that, in time, will help create buildings that engage better with the user and with their surroundings.

The design is carried out through collective way of thinking and working that focuses on precision. For each project, hundreds of 3D and small-large scale models are developed to test the design decisions. This detail-oriented approach means clients can be confident that the project is executed to its finest detail through all project phases.

EAA constantly seeks to improve its methods through technological advancements and find new ways of sculpting light and materials, minimize the environmental impact, and articulate the design from the start through producing details that work and represent the final building. Every building EAA designs is a unique work combining intellectual and artistic sensitivity tempered by the tradition and culture from which they spring. Significant acknowledgement of EAA's work can be listed as;

2018 Sancaklar Mosque, RIBA International Prize
      Istanbul Museum of Painting&Sculpture, MIPIM/ AR Future, Cultural Regeneration Category Winner
2017 Cukurova Regional Airport, The Plan Award
      Mecidiyekoy Mixed Use Complex, AAP-American Architecture Prize
      Goksu Residences, WAF 'Future Residential' Category Winner
2016 Sancaklar Mosque, German Design Award
      Dalaman International Airport II, Sign of the City Award
2015 Sancaklar Mosque, European Union Prize for Architecture Finalist, Archdaily Religious Building of the Year, Designs of the Year Finalist, Design Museum, London
2014 Antakya Museum Hotel, WAF 'Future Leisure Led' Category Winner
2012 AGU Sumer Campus Planning, WAF 'Future Education' Category Winner
2011 RDKM-Raif Dinckok Cultural Center, Cityscape Dubai Awards, Completed Leisure Buildings Category Winner
2010 Ipekyol Textile Factory, Aga Khan Award for Architecture
2008 Zorlu Center, European & African Property Awards, Cityscape Dubai Awards for Special and Master Planning
2005 Minicity Theme Park, European Union Prize for Contemporary Architecture-Mies Van der Rohe Award

On the cover: Sancaklar Mosque, photograph by Cemal Emden

We thank all copyright owners for their kind permission to reproduce their material. Should, despite our intensive research, any person entitled to rights have been overlooked, legitimate claims shall be compensated within the usual provisions.

Texts: Emre Arolat, Aaron Betsky
Design: EAA - Emre Arolat Architecture New York
Design production: Ozge Ertoptamis, Junggu Kim
Coordination: Ozge Ertoptamis
Copyediting: Ozge Ertoptamis
Translation: Victoria Holbrook
Project Coordinator: Kirby Anderson

Publishers of Architecture, Art, and Design
Gordon Goff: Publisher
www.oroeditions.com
info@oroeditions.com
Published by ORO Editions

Copyright © Emre Arolat Architecture 2019
Text and Images © Emre Arolat Architecture 2019

All rights reserved. No part of this book may be reproduced, stored in a retrieval system, or transmitted in any form or by any means, including electronic, mechanical, photocopying of microfilming, recording, or otherwise (except that copying permitted by Sections 107 and 108 of the U.S. Copyright Law and except by reviewers for the public press) without written permission from the publisher.

You must not circulate this book in any other binding or cover and you must impose this same condition on any acquirer.

10 9 8 7 6 5 4 3 2 1 First Edition

Library of Congress data available upon request. World Rights: Available

ISBN: 978-1-941806-38-8

Color Separations and Printing: ORO Group Ltd.
Printed in China.

International Distribution: www.oroeditions.com/distribution

ORO Editions makes a continuous effort to minimize the overall carbon footprint of its publications. As part of this goal, ORO Editions, in association with Global ReLeaf, arranges to plant trees to replace those used in the manufacturing of the paper produced for its books. Global ReLeaf is an international campaign run by American Forests, one of the world's oldest nonprofit conservation organizations. Global ReLeaf is American Forests' education and action program that helps individuals, organizations, agencies, and corporations improve the local and global environment by planting and caring for trees.